The World of Work

Written by
Silvie Sanža

Illustrated by
Milan Starý

SCRIBO
_a_ SALARIYA _imprint_

Hi!

My name is Alfie and I'm a dog. I was just looking up at the Moon and suddenly I thought 'Why don't I go up there to take a proper look?'

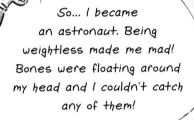

So... I became an astronaut. Being weightless made me mad! Bones were floating around my head and I couldn't catch any of them!

I decided to try something a little calmer. It was peaceful in the art studio and I liked the smell of oil paints ... but I didn't like having to wash it out of my fur every evening!

I started to hunt for a different profession. The next thing I know, I'm a detective. I found a lot of lost sausages and was looking forward to eating them but—being an agent of the law—I had to give them all back...!

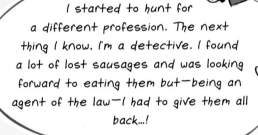

That made me really hungry! I had no money so I started working at a shopping mall but the tinkling of cash registers gave me a headache. We dogs have really sensitive hearing, you know.

Turns out that choosing the right job isn't easy at all! I need to go and research the kind of places I like. Come with me if you want, and take a look at lots of different professions.

Let's go!

List of professions

The professions in bold are described in detail in the book.

What's it like working in a...
Theater?

Lighting technician

"Which play are you doing...?!"

Dramatist

"This way, please"

Usher

Actr[ess]

Director

Audio engineer

"Awww!"

"Wow!"

Prompter

Playwright

First aid attendant

Lighting technician

Checkroom attendant

Playwright

A playwright writes plays. He creates its storyline, and the speeches that each actor will say on the stage.

I create the stories and characters that will become a play.

Director

A director runs the entire theater production, making all decisions about actors, sound, lighting, costumes, and set design. It is the director who decides what will happen on stage, helps the actors to rehearse their parts, and gives orders. This is how a theater performance is created.

Theater designer

This job is about designing the stage and costumes in a way that will best express the character of the play. The designer draws sketches for the seamstresses and technicians who will create the costumes, furniture, and set design in their workrooms.

SEAMSTRESS

Stagehand

It is the job of the stagehands to change the stage into a castle, street scene, or lake if required. During the performance they bring any props and furniture on or off the stage.

Welcome. Come in, the performance is about to begin!

Dramatist

A dramatist researches interesting stage plays or ideas. If a selected script is not completely suitable, the dramatist may edit some of the lines, update a storyline or setting, or perhaps make some character changes. A dramatist interprets and adapts scripts to suit the specific needs of a director or theater.

I choose which plays my theater presents.

Actor

Actors need to be talented. Simply memorizing a part isn't enough. An actor must be able to convincingly portray a character in a play.

Audio engineer

Additional atmosphere is created for each performance with music or various sound effects played from an audio engineer's audio mixer.

Lighting technician

In large theaters, there are a vast range of lights aimed at the stage. A lighting technician controls all the lighting using a special mixer.

Stage manager

Stage managers make sure that everything takes place at exactly the right moment. Actors are called in time for their stage entrance and props must be checked for each scene.

Prompter

If an actor forgets any lines on stage, it is a prompter's job to whisper it.

Make-up artist

A make-up artist is responsible for creating the make-up that best expresses each stage character.

Hair stylist

Hair stylists can make wigs, or create whatever hair style a character needs.

Fisherman

A fish farmer is in charge of a pond in terms of the breeding, processing, and selling of fish. A fisherman, on the other hand, enjoys fishing as a pastime.

Fish farmer

Fish don't speak ...but I can still understand them.

Agronomist

An agronomist decides which crops to plant, how to take care of them, when to reap the harvest, and how to process it.

My apples are packed full of vitamin C.

Sunflowers...or potatoes? I can tell you when to plant them!

Gardener

A gardener cares for ornamental plants, vegetables, and orchards.

Everyone knows that sheep need pastures and ducks need ponds, but there's so much more to know!

Forester

Foresters looks after forests. They check if trees are healthy, and decide when trees need to be thinned out, or how many new seedlings to plant.

Livestock specialist

This occupation requires an exhaustive knowledge of farm animals. A livestock specialist supervises feeding, looks after livestock's health and reproduction, and runs production, mainly of meat and dairy products.

Lumberjack

Once it's been decided that a tree must be cut down, the job is entrusted to a lumberjack.

I know every tree in this forest. Bark beetles shudder when they see me coming.

Veterinarian

A veterinarian, or "vet", is an animal doctor who performs medical examinations, treats animals for illnesses and injuries, and helps them to give birth. A vet will also check whether a farm's products are hygienic and harmless.

Beekeeper

A beekeeper cares for bees. This job includes managing beehives, renewing bee colonies, breeding queen bees, or processing the products made by bees, especially propolis, honey, and wax.

Farmer

Being the head of a farm, the farmer's role mainly consists of cultivating the land to grow corn, wheat, and other crops, or breeding livestock and poultry. A farmer also needs a good business mind in order to find customers to buy the farm's products.

Gamekeeper

Gamekeepers keep vermin down, watch out for poachers in the district, and check for any signs of animal infections. They may give extra food to some forest animals, especially during winter.

Tractor driver

No farm can survive without a tractor. A tractor driver doesn't only drive it, but repairs it, too.

Logger

And if it's impossible to reach a place by tractor, a wagon is used. A logger holds the reins and tends to the horses before and after work. He feeds them, cleans their stalls, and takes care of the harnesses.

Navigator

Day or night, navigators constantly monitor the ship's position. A navigator must plan the route, inform the captain about any changes or imminent dangers, and keep the voyage schedule on time.

Able seaman

Able seamen perform a range of manual work like ship maintenance, painting, or minor repairs.

Radio officer

It is a radio officer's duty to maintain communication at all times between the ship and mainland, and with other vessels.

Cabin steward

Cabin stewards clean the passengers' cabins and change their towels and bedding.

Ship's captain

A ship's captain is responsible for ensuring a safe voyage, choosing a suitable route, and commanding the crew. The captain is in charge of everything on the ship and must be aware of navy law, and be a capable manager.

Deck steward

Deck stewards keep all decks in good order.

Activities coordinator

This job is about planning entertainment for the passengers throughout the voyage by organizing a varied social, cultural, and sports program.

Tour guide

When the ship stops in port, a tour guide can take passengers for planned trips and excursions.

Fitness instructor

Passengers who want more physical activity can turn to a fitness instructor who organizes dancing, yoga, and aerobic classes. An instructor may offer individual work-outs and exercises, and can also give advice on a good diet.

Lifeguard

It is a lifeguard's duty to keep a close eye on the safety of passengers in the swimming pool. They are on standby in case anyone gets into trouble in the pool or is in need of first aid.

Ship's engineer

It's a ship engineer's job to prevent any malfunction occurring during a voyage. Engineers have to make sure that all technical devices are fully functional, all engines are properly lubricated and cooled, batteries are charged, and the rudders are in good condition.

Air traffic controller

Air traffic controllers, in the control tower, use radar to track the exact position of planes that are currently sharing the airspace. They are responsible for authorizing all takeoffs and landings.

Flight attendant

A flight attendant's job includes a lot of traveling, day or night, and at weekends. They must ensure the passenger's safety and comfort at all times, and be able to deal with stressful situations. A second language is very beneficial.

Customs officer

When international passengers land they must go through customs clearance and passport control. Customs officers make sure that passengers don't try to import any illegal or dangerous goods like guns, drugs, tobacco, alcohol, or protected plants or animals.

Meteorologist

Bad weather can create problems for airplanes, so a meteorologist keeps a close eye on air pressure, wind, cloud conditions, and air temperature. Weather reports are submitted to all pilots.

Pilot

The main part of a pilot's job is flying a plane, but they are responsible for many other things, too. A pilot must keep check on the fuel gauge, ensure all devices are fully functional, plan the plane's flight route, and communicate with air traffic control.

Ornithologist

Ornithologists keep watch for any birds near to the airport. They try to scare them away, sometimes with the help of trained birds of prey.

It is highly dangerous if a plane collides with birds.

Airport manager

An airport manager is responsible for running the airport and all its employees. It is the manager's responsibility to oversee the state of runways, coordinate the refueling of gas tanks, and the loading up of planes. A manager must solve all problems that could possibly occur at the airport.

Unload the plane, re-load it. Fill up the tank and let's go!

Everything has to work perfectly—small mistakes may cost lives!

Flight mechanic

Flight mechanics are troubleshooters who carry a great responsibility on their shoulders. They must ensure that all the plane's mechanical systems are in excellent working order. As aircraft designers create more intricate and complex mechanisms, the flight mechanics must constantly update their knowledge.

Hotel manager

Hotels have lots of staff to attend to the needs of their many guests. Hotel managers are in charge of every aspect of the hotel's staff and service, and they manage and plan bookings with travel agencies or individual guests. They make sure that everything is running well so that guests enjoy their stay and will want to come back.

A wedding party...forty rooms? Of course. I'll make your reservation.

I, Alphonso, will make your stomach fall in love with my hotel!!

Chef

Chefs create new recipes, decide on a hotel's menus, order prime quality ingredients for cooking, and direct a team of cooks in the kitchen.

Welcome to our hotel, sir. Would you prefer a room with a balcony?

Receptionist

A receptionist welcomes new guests, books them into the hotel, and assigns rooms and room keys. Receptionists have to deal with each guest's wishes...or objections. It is their job to make the occupants of their hotel feel at home.

I am the first and last person you will meet at this hotel.

Porter

Doorman

It is a doorman's job to open the entrance door for guests coming in or leaving the hotel. It is his responsibility to create a good first impression to all guests. He summons porters to help carry the guests' luggage up to their room.

Waiters and waitresses have to set tables, carry food from the kitchen to the dining room, and serve meals correctly. They need to be efficient, have a pleasant demeanor and a good memory for each table's orders. A sommelier advises guests with their wine choice, and is in charge of the hotel's wine cellar.

Wine waiter

Waitress

Waiter

We're here to give you excellent service.

I'll make your life a little bit sweeter.

Confectioner

Pies, cakes, and desserts . . . a master confectioner can bake delicious treats that will melt in your mouth. A confectioner needs good recipe ideas, an artistic eye, and a light touch to create sweet courses that both look and taste heavenly.

Hotel security

The hotel security staff ensures the safety of all guests and their belongings. They will deal with troublemakers and prevent any theft. If anything does go wrong they will take on the role of hotel detective.

Stop thief...that briefcase belongs to Mr Black!

I'll add your initials to this cappuchino, Madam.

Bartender

Good bartenders must know how to make a wide variety of cocktails, and be able to create brand new ones, too. Their job is to prepare all drinks for the guests.

Going in or going out...? That is the question. Heavy luggage is no problem for me.

Barista

The bar is shared with baristas, expert coffee-makers who have an extensive knowledge about all types of coffee and coffee beverages.

Cardiologist

Surgeon

Medicine is one of the toughest subjects to study because the learning process is never-ending. Once graduated, a doctor will choose an area of medicine to specialize in. A cardiologist treats all forms of heart disease. A doctor who performs surgery is called a surgeon, so a cardiac surgeon operates on patients with heart problems.

Nurse

Nurses look after their patients in many ways. They check blood pressure, temperature, take blood samples, and assist with examinations, surgery and childbirth.

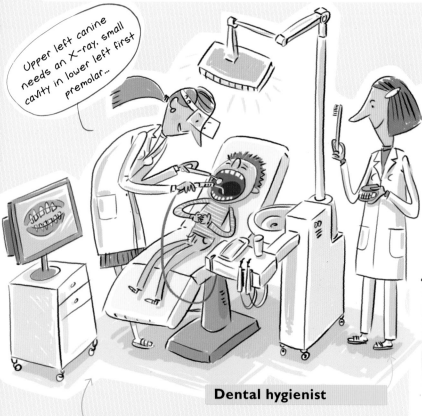

Dental hygienist

Dentist

A dentist looks after teeth and gums, provides preventative care and, as a last resort, will remove teeth. A dental hygienist checks oral hygiene and advises patients how to brush their teeth and gums correctly. Both try to prevent the occurrence of dental problems.

Optometrist

When a patient goes to the optician, it is an optometrist who tests his eyesight to determine the strength of lenses or contact lens needed. The optometrist can also help with the choice of frames.

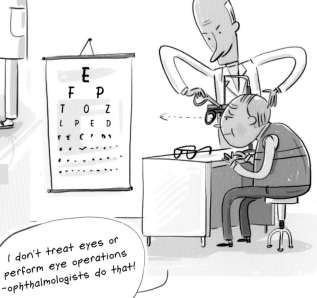

Pediatrician

People don't just visit their doctor when they're sick. They may need advice, an inoculation, or an examination. A pediatrician is a children's doctor who treats only babies and children.

Physiotherapist

Physiotherapists help patients to improve or correct an existing physical disability, or those caused through injury. They teach patients how to strengthen that part of their body through exercise and massage. Physiotherapists can help rehabilitate people who have very serious problems.

Midwife

Midwives take care of mothers-to-be and help them to give birth, either at home or in a maternity ward. They may also help mothers to look after their newborn babies during their first weeks of life.

Pharmacist

Pharmacists supply us with medicines, recommend the correct usage and may suggest ways to avoid any potential side-effects. They also develop and produce these medications. Pharmacists often advise people about their ailments, too.

What are you looking for... Romance? Thriller? Gardening? Horror?

Bookseller

Good booksellers must be well read to keep up with new book releases and bestsellers. Having a good working knowledge of a wide range of subjects means that they can recommend books to their customers, whatever the subject: history, thrillers, art, travel...

Truck driver

Truck drivers often travel long distances. They must be experienced, reliable drivers who can manage simple repairs, and deliver goods on time.

Phew, the traffic was murder today. I thought I would be late!

Warehouseman

When a truck driver delivers goods to a store, a warehouseman checks to see if it's fresh and intact before accepting it. He also keeps the warehouse clean and organized.

I may be out of sight but I keep the store up and running!

Let me help you choose the perfect flowers for that special occasion.

Window dresser

Window dressers need an imaginative and artistic approach to make a shop window eye-catching. Sometimes they decorate the entire store in order to advertise a new collection or special offer.

I can attract customers—just leave it to me!

Florist

Need a beautiful wedding bouquet, flowers, or plants for a special gift, or perhaps to decorate a room for a celebration? Florists know everything about flowers and can advise you which ones look good together and how best to care for them.

Banker

If you want to buy a house, invest money, or even save it, a banker can suggest the best ways for you to do so. Bankers are well aware of what other banks, besides their own, have to offer and can guide you to the best solutions.

Cashier

A cashier works out the total cost of purchases, takes payment, and will wrap or put a customer's items into a bag for them.

Store assistant

Store assistants know what goods their store has to offer. They help customers to find the size they require and may offer some alternative choices or perhaps accessories.

Ice cream seller

Ice cream sellers are experts at conjuring up mouth-watering flavors to cool you down on a hot summer's day… or just brighten up any day of the year! They need to have a good knowledge of recipes in order to turn fruit, cream, and chocolate into delicious ice creams and sorbets.

Teacher

Teachers need to have a good understanding of their subject. However, being good at math, science or foreign languages is not enough—they must also have a talent for teaching. Only good teachers can pass on their knowledge to others.

I love experimenting!

I love numbers...

Flora and Fauna!

History... fascinating!

Basketball – my favorite!

Special educational needs teacher

Some children find it difficult to learn in the same way as others do. A special educational needs teacher has a wider understanding of different approaches to learning which may suit some children's needs better. Not all children learn in the same way.

Let's do it another way, shall we—there are lots of ways to learn!

Principal

A principal has to keep the whole school running smoothly and efficiently. The principal is in charge of all teachers and other employees of the school and makes decisions about how the school is run to provide a good education for all children.

Secretary

The secretary organizes schedules, writes letters, arranges meetings, and updates the principal with any necessary information.

Tell me what interests you and I'll tell you what you could become.

It helps to talk about problems—perhaps I can help?

Janitor

A janitor takes care of the school building. He keeps it clean, tidy, and safe for the teachers and children. It's his job to perform everyday maintenance and minor repairs.

School counselor

School counselors help pupils to choose which subjects they might want to study. They can also recommend suitable professions and offer further guidance.

School psychologist

Everybody has a problem once in a while. That's why schools employ their own psychologists to listen to troubled pupils. They try to help them resolve problems.

Tell me what you need and I'll help you find it!

After a long day's hard work—it's good to have some fun!

Librarian

The school librarian is in charge of the library. It is the librarian's job to catalog all the books, order new ones, and make sure that the pupils and teachers can find the best books available and make good use of the library.

Class assistant

Before school starts and at the end of each day, class assistants may organize breakfast clubs and various after-school clubs. Sometimes they help teachers supervise during break time, or they may review pupils' homework.

Emergency call handlers

Emergency call handlers must have sufficient medical knowledge to make swift decisions. On receiving a distress call, they will quickly find out exactly what has happened in order to pass on all relevant information to the emergency services. They will advise the caller how to take care of the injured person until the emergency services arrive.

It's my job to send the right type of rescue to the right place at the right time.

Stranded on a mountain? Buried in an avalanche? Lost on a mountain trail? It's all in a day's work for us!

Mountain rescue service

A mountain rescue squad has to cope with a variety of rescue situations. Its crew members undergo training in mountain climbing, skiing, and flying in order to be able to find people in remote areas, offer them first aid, and transport them to a location that paramedics can reach.

My dog can see, hear, and sniff out anything!

Dog handler

Dog handlers and dogs work together as a professional team in many types of operations: helping to prevent and detect crime, finding lost or missing persons, searching for explosives or illegal drugs, and guarding people or properties.

...or a reliable horse gets us to places cars can't reach.

Police

Investigations often take place in terrain that is difficult to reach. Then the police force will use motorbikes, bicycles, or horses to get there. The mounted police officer training is extremely difficult and includes dressage, horse jumping, and horse control in stressful situations.

A bike...

Firefighter

Besides putting out fires, firefighters also rescue people who find themselves in dangerous situations. Firefighters often save people from great heights, flooded locations, burning houses, or wrecked cars.

Paramedic

When medical attention is needed urgently, an ambulance is sent to help. An ambulance crew mostly consists of a paramedic and a driver. A paramedic's training is similar to that of a doctor, so a patient's needs can be dealt with promptly and safely without a doctor's supervision.

Diver

Diving is a very demanding profession. Divers must be in peak physical condition, be excellent swimmers, and have no fear underwater. They may dive in search of missing people or evidence, and may also take part in anti-drug or anti-terrorist operations.

Bomb disposal officer

When a suspicious object is found, a bomb disposal squad must be summoned to identify whether or not it is a dangerous explosive device. If it is, a bomb disposal officer will either defuse or destroy the device to make it safe.

Painter

Bright colors or pale shades … a painter can mix every possible hue. They can paint a property's walls, ceilings, and woodwork as requested.

My most reliable assistants are my paintbrushes, rollers, a bucket, and a ladder!

I can design a dream house, a concert hall, a train station or… a school?

Architect

Architects are part-artists and part-designers. They also need a wide knowledge of all the technical aspects of construction to ensure that the finished building is safe, attractive, and suitable for purpose.

Site manager

A site manager recruits a team of tradesmen and is responsible for the whole building project being completed safely, as planned, and on time. They must understand building plans and regulations, resolve any problems, and supervise all aspects of construction, including the safety of all the workers.

Landscape architect

Landscape architects design the layout of gardens and parks. They know which plants should be planted in shaded or sunny positions, and can advise how to plant out flowerbeds so they are interesting throughout the year.

The roofer is in the basement…and the plumber's on the roof? It should be the other way around!

Ah… these perennials would be better over there!

Project architect

Project architects develop the architect's designs into meticulous plans that detail, for example, where the water pipes are to be laid, and where the electrical wiring and heating systems must go.

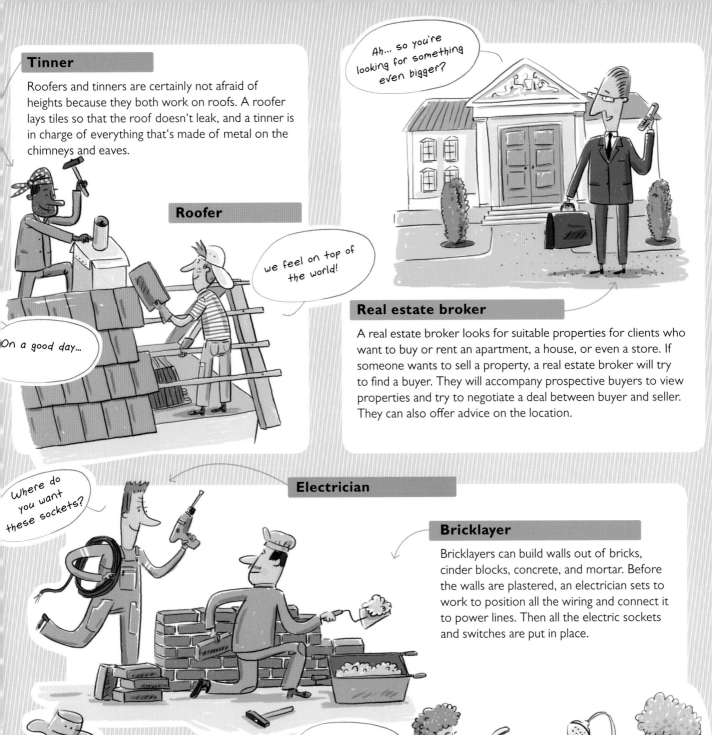

Tinner

Roofers and tinners are certainly not afraid of heights because they both work on roofs. A roofer lays tiles so that the roof doesn't leak, and a tinner is in charge of everything that's made of metal on the chimneys and eaves.

Roofer

Ah... so you're looking for something even bigger?

we feel on top of the world!

On a good day...

Real estate broker

A real estate broker looks for suitable properties for clients who want to buy or rent an apartment, a house, or even a store. If someone wants to sell a property, a real estate broker will try to find a buyer. They will accompany prospective buyers to view properties and try to negotiate a deal between buyer and seller. They can also offer advice on the location.

Electrician

Where do you want these sockets?

Bricklayer

Bricklayers can build walls out of bricks, cinder blocks, concrete, and mortar. Before the walls are plastered, an electrician sets to work to position all the wiring and connect it to power lines. Then all the electric sockets and switches are put in place.

Now you can have a nice swim!

Plumber

A plumber is indispensable. Without one, no water would flow in or out of a property. A plumber can lay water pipes, install sinks, baths, showers, and faucets, and do many plumbing repairs.

I'm aware of all arrivals and departures and everyone working at my station.

Station manager

A station manager is responsible for the entire rail station and its staff. A manager must ensure the smooth running of all train arrivals and departures so no delays or accidents occur.

Train driver

A train driver ensures the train's safe arrival at its destination. Before a journey begins, all equipment and engines must be checked and the control center contacted for up to date information regarding any route changes or problems.

Trains don't have steering wheels—I operate it with a control panel.

Signal disk… is the proper name for my so-called 'flapper'

Rail carriage and wagon inspector

A rail carriage and wagon inspector conducts technical inspections of wagons and carriages to identify any defects. Brakes and other vital parts are checked before the train is judged fit to go. If any fault is discovered, a rail vehicle mechanic must be called in to fix it.

Train dispatcher

A train dispatcher is one of the most important people at a train station. Dispatchers are responsible for the safety of rail passengers. They authorize all arrivals and departures using a whistle and signal disk.

Rail vehicle mechanic

Before the train departs, I have to check that it is safe to do so.

Operational planner

Scheduling the arrival and departure of hundreds of trains is no laughing matter. Trains must come and go without too much delay and allow enough time for passengers to get safely on and off. And … of course, trains mustn't collide! A planner uses specialized computer software to make this complicated process a little bit easier.

Conductor

Train conductors, or guards, check passengers' tickets and can advise them about arrival times and when and where to change trains. They can issue tickets onboard, and make sure everything is in order and that passengers are safe and comfortable.

Track maintenance supervisor

Trains cannot travel without tracks. It's the job of a track maintenance supervisor to inspect the tracks and attachments to ensure they are in perfect working order. If any defects are found, a track maintenance worker will be called in to weld or make adjustments to carry out the track repairs.

Train shunter

A train shunter makes sure that each train consists of the correct number of cars, and that the train is on the right track and facing the correct way. The shunter also ensures that no train moves before a train dispatcher allows it to leave.

Track maintenance worker

Ballet dancer

It takes an enormous amount of hard work for a ballet dancer to be capable of all the graceful moves, leaps, and pirouettes required. Ballet dancers practice many hours every day in order to stay in top physical condition for their performances.

Composer

Librettist

A librettist and a composer must collaborate on ballet or opera performances. A librettist writes the words, called the libretto. A composer then composes and writes music for it. Composers often play one or more instruments but that isn't necessary. They must understand how instruments will sound both individually and played together.

Choirmaster

A choirmaster or mistress is in charge of the choir. They choose the choir's repertoire, study new compositions, lead rehearsals, and assign solo parts.

Singer

In order to be able to sing an entire opera or concert, singers must have a good ear for music, a beautiful voice, and be prepared to practice a lot! A voice teacher helps them to strengthen their vocal cords, and perfect their vocal techniques.

Ballet master

Ballet masters or mistresses are in charge of all the ballet dancers. They decide which ballets will be performed and who will dance the solo parts. When a new performance is being practiced, they take charge of rehearsals and are responsible for studying every dance part.

Conductor

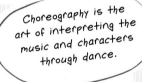

Despite not playing any musical instrument, the conductor is still the most important person in the whole orchestra. Conductors have to study each composition with the musicians, practice with them, and conduct them during concerts by showing them whose turn it is to play, in which tempo and at what volume.

Répétiteur

A répétiteur is the piano accompanist for dance or singing practice. Répétiteurs are indispensable when solo singers and choirs are rehearsing, as it would be too costly and complicated to summon a whole orchestra for each and every rehearsal.

oice teacher

Choreographer

A ballet or opera choreographer will decide how the dancers and actors will move or dance to the composer's music, and participates in all rehearsals.

What's it like working in a...
Film Studio?

Propman

"Where's the snow? We need snow NOW!"

Production designer

"Ten hot dogs, please"

Caterer

"Whimper"

Alfie

Production manager

Actress

Director of photography

Camera operator

Hair stylist

Make-up artist

"Shouldn't I be green?"

"We ran out of green"

Actor

Sound engineer

Boom operator

Production designer

Production designers create the visual styling of a movie. They decide on the design style for the sets, locations, costumes, props and lighting. They work closely with the director and producer.

Scripts are divided into 'shots' rather than chapters.

Screenwriter

Screenwriters will either create their own stories for movies, or interpret other people's ideas or books. They need imagination to write good movie scripts, and to develop believable plots and characters. Screenwriters thoroughly research all background material and must be prepared to rewrite if necessary.

Isn't it too modern to be medieval?

Script supervisor

Script supervisors need a good memory for detail to make sure that a plot doesn't contain any mistakes. Often, scenes aren't filmed in order, or even on the same day, so scene continuity is their responsibility. They must ensure that details remain identical throughout the shoot.

Wait a minute... that hat had daisies on it in the last scene!

Producer

Producers decide which movie will be filmed. Then they raise funds for its production, plan a budget, and choose its crew, including its director, production manager, director of photography, sound engineer and editor.

Camera operator

Director of photography

A director of photography (DOP) determines how a scene will be shot: the camera angle, the lighting, and the length of each individual shot. The assistant camera operator then operates the camera according to the DOP's directions.

Production manager

Before shooting starts, everything must be carefully planned. A production manager prepares the shooting schedule and has to make sure that everything proceeds as planned.

Stunt performer

Stuntmen and women stand in for actors by performing their action scenes. They can run, fight, climb, jump from great heights, dive, fence, drive fast cars —they have to be prepared to do practically anything.

Movie editor

A movie editor combines individual shots into the final version of a movie. They have to compose the plot, sound and images in a way that creates a coherent and engaging movie.

Journalist

Journalists can suggest topics for publication, but they must be able to write an article on any subject required by the magazine. They can do background research online or in books, conduct interviews, or go into the field to report on a story.

Editor-in-chief

Before any work begins, the Editor-in-chief will decide on which subjects to feature in the upcoming issue. An Editor-in-chief doesn't have to write articles, but needs good management skills to run the whole editorial office, supervise the budget, and communicate with all other colleagues.

Proofreader

Before any issue is finally sent to be printed, a proofreader will check each article for clarity, accuracy, and any overlooked spelling, grammar, or stylistic mistakes.

Interpreter

If a journalist has to conduct an interview with a foreign movie star or visiting dignitary, an interpreter is called in to help. They must have a good grasp of the interviewee's language in order to interpret their responses and accurately translate it from one language to another.

Editor

Before finished articles are positioned on magazine pages, they must be edited. An editor judges the content for quality, may cut text length if necessary, and corrects any stylistic problems.

Webmaster

Web designer

No modern magazine can do without its own webpage. A web designer designs it, a programmer puts it into operation, and a webmaster makes sure it's up to date and works smoothly.

Graphic designer

A graphic designer typesets the finished text and images, and uses a specialized computer program to lay out pages in the way that they will appear in the printed magazine.

Photographer

A photographer supplies photographs to accompany magazine articles. Subjects range widely so a photographer might be photographing models on a catwalk one day, snapping pictures of social events on another, or perhaps documenting a historical event.

Subscription service

Advertising agent

To help cover the costs of creating and printing each issue, a magazine reserves some pages to sell as advertising space. It employs sales people to negotiate the cost of placing prospective ads and to deal with magazine subscriptions.

Exhibition designer

There's more to making an exhibition engaging than just placing precious objects in showcases. An exhibition designer needs creative flair to visualize how to make the most of an exhibition space. Interesting displays may include innovative graphics, props, lighting, and perhaps even sound.

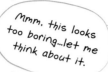

Restorer

Restorers painstakingly fix many damaged artifacts like sculptures, paintings, ceramics, pottery, or valuable carpets. A restorer needs to have great skill, patience, and an eye for detail. Before restorers set to work, they carefully research how an object was originally made so they can restore it accurately.

Mineralogist

Entomologist

There are at least three hundred and fifty thousand types of insect in the world. Does anyone know them all? A museum's entomologist manages its insect collection and even knows about insects that are extinct! Likewise, anthropologists study humans, botanists study plants, and mineralogists study minerals. Each museum employs numerous specialists like these.

Anthropologist

Botanist

Curator

Museums can't afford to collect all works of art. It is a curator's job to decide which artifacts should be acquired to enhance the museum's existing collections. A curator needs an extensive knowledge of one or more areas of art, natural science, or history to lead the team of assistants who care for the collections. Curators may loan items to or from other museums and they plan exhibitions.

Archeologist

Knowledge of languages like Latin or ancient Greek can help archeologists to date and interpret objects recovered from an excavation. They take part in field expeditions and examine objects to assess their age and origins before preserving and documenting them.

Every tiny piece is important.

Now this painting will last another few hundred years.

Conservator

Conservators manage, preserve, treat and care for museum artifacts. They monitor environments where collections are stored or displayed to prevent light, heat, or moisture causing any further deterioration. They are experts who use scientific methods to examine objects in order to understand the best way to restore or preserve them.

See if you can do your own version now.

Press agent

A press agent's role comes into play when new exhibitions are planned. Press agents try to make sure that the upcoming event is well publicized so that as many people as possible know that an exhibition is coming. They write articles about it for newspapers and give interviews to radio and TV stations.

Guide

A museum guide will take visitors around an exhibition to tell them more about the various exhibits. A guide can answer individual questions and give a fuller explanation. They are particularly helpful for groups of schoolchildren.

This unique exhibition will take visitors back in time.

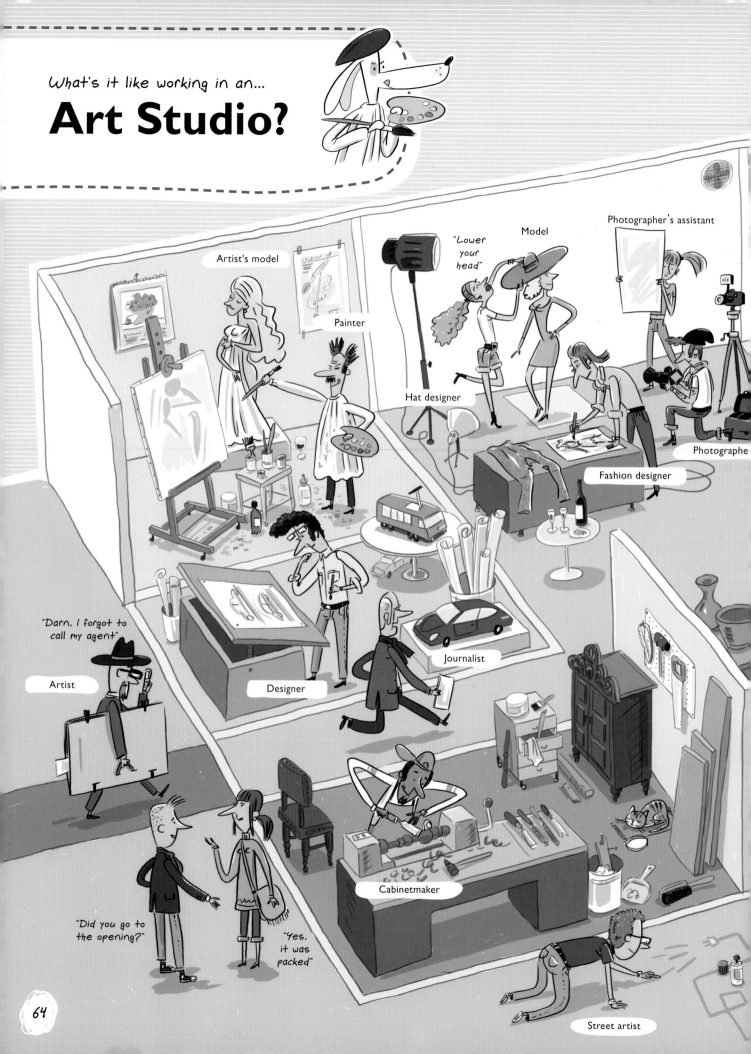

What's it like working in an...
Art Studio?

Artist's model

Painter

"Lower your head"

Model

Photographer's assistant

Hat designer

Photographe

Fashion designer

"Darn, I forgot to call my agent"

Artist

Designer

Journalist

Cabinetmaker

"Did you go to the opening?"

"Yes, it was packed"

Street artist

Cabinetmaker

Cabinetmakers are skilled craftsmen who can create beautifully carved furniture out of wood. They make highly original pieces by hand, either using their own designs or other people's. They will also repair and restore antique furniture.

Painter

There are many painting techniques and skills for artists to learn. A good painter needs to have an eye for color, composition, and proportion. The originality of a painter's work often comes down to technique and an inquisitive mind, which makes some paintings stand out from others.

Performance artist

Performance artists can include visual artists, actors, photographers, dancers, singers … or any combination. It is an unconventional genre that is usually presented "live." It is often spontaneous and improvized but may also be rehearsed carefully beforehand. It can involve one or more participants and sometimes relies on audience participation.

Illustrator

Illustrators draw and paint images for books, magazines and webpages. They need to have good drawing skills and a sense of color. Illustrators usually create illustrations 'on demand' to suit a client's needs but may also create and illustrate their own projects.

Sculptor

Sculptors usually express themselves in 3D, often carving sculptures out of wood or stone, or by casting metal, or using plastics. The work of a sculptor is just as variable as a painter: some produce very realistic work while others prefer to work in a purely abstract way.

Fashion designer

Fashion designers have the skill to combine color, fabric, and shape, transforming them into fabulous outfits. They need to know how to make and cut patterns, understand how fabrics will drape, and have the necessary sewing techniques to be able to construct their finished designs.

You can have whatever hat you want—I make them all by hand.

Hat designer

Goldsmith

Goldsmiths design, make, and sell items made from gold. They work with a variety of metals, set precious gems, and make and repair jewelry. Goldsmiths know how to solder, shape, and polish precious metals, and need good eyesight to be able to do highly detailed work when required.

A lot of my ideas for shapes come from nature.

Designer

Designers can create new trends in fashion. They come up with different ideas to create a new and unusual look to everyday things like glasses, chairs, vacuum cleaners, cars, in fact, anything. A designer needs a good eye for shape, color, and construction techniques to make sure that the finished design not only looks good but is functional and practical.

Astronaut

An engineer, physicist, biologist, or mathematician can become an astronaut, but it takes many years of education and experience even to qualify for training. As well as an extensive knowledge of their professions, they must also be in peak physical and psychological condition. Before being allowed to undergo space training they have to pass many tests, for example, managing to swim across a pool wearing a cumbersome spacesuit.

Life support technician

In case of emergency, each astronaut is equipped with his own special helmet, suit, oxygen mask, parachute, and survival kit. This equipment is regularly checked by a life support technician, who also teaches the crew how to eject, parachute, and land on ground or water.

Commander

A commander must complete at least a thousand hours as a jet pilot before taking control of the cockpit of a spacecraft. The commander is the captain of the spacecraft and is responsible for the safety of the entire ship and its crew, and the success of their mission.

Go and dry yourself and then we'll try the zero gravity simulation.

Payload specialist

Payload specialists are technical experts who accompany specific payloads into space or oversee certain experiments. Payload specialists are generally research scientists or experts from a scientific institution rather than trained astronauts.

It's grown three inches in four days.

Flight engineer

Flight engineers monitor the functionality of all devices and systems present on the spacecraft. They also assist the pilot and the commander in managing the ship.

Mission specialist

A mission specialist works with the commander and pilot. They have detailed knowledge of the spacecraft's systems and mission requirements. They can perform activities out in open space and operate a Canadarm—the spacecraft's long manipulation arm that is used to discharge or recover cargo.

Launch director

A launch director makes the final, crucial decision as to whether a spacecraft launch should proceed or not. They monitor everything up to this point including weather and all technical aspects of the spacecraft. Only when the launch director decides that a launch is safe to go can the departure procedure commence.

Flight controller

Space missions are under constant monitoring by teams of flight controllers on Earth. At the mission control center, numerous specialized flight controllers check the spacecraft's technical equipment, and the health and physical condition of its crew.

Aerospace engineer

An aerospace engineer's job is to develop the devices required by research scientists in space. This entails mechanical design, producing prototypes, testing, and bringing the finished apparatus into operation.

Phew, there's a lot of interesting jobs
in the world. But you know what?
I think I like being a dog most of all...
What about you?
Do you know what you want to be
when you grow up?

Published in MMXVII by
Scribo, an imprint of
The Salariya Book Company Ltd
25 Marlborough Place, Brighton BN1 1UB
www.salariya.com

ISBN: 978-1-911242-87-1

SALARIYA

1 3 5 7 9 8 6 4 2
© Designed by B4U Publishing, 2014
A member of Albatros Media Group
Author: Silvie Sanša
Illustrations: Milan Starý
www.b4upublishing.com
All rights reserved.
Translation rights arranged though JNJ Agency.
English text © The Salariya Book Company Ltd MMXVII

A CIP catalogue record for this book is available
from the British Library.

Printed and bound in China.